John Logan

A Review of the Principal Charges Against Warren Hastings,

Esquire,

Late Governor General of Bengal

John Logan

A Review of the Principal Charges Against Warren Hastings, Esquire,
Late Governor General of Bengal

ISBN/EAN: 9783337012755

Printed in Europe, USA, Canada, Australia, Japan

Cover: Foto ©ninafisch / pixelio.de

More available books at **www.hansebooks.com**

A REVIEW

OF THE

PRINCIPAL CHARGES

AGAINST

WARREN HASTINGS Esquire,
Late Governor General of Bengal.

LONDON:

PRINTED FOR JOHN STOCKDALE, OPPOSITE
BURLINGTON-HOUSE, PICCADILLY; AND
JOHN MURRAY, FLEET-STREET.
MDCCLXXXVIII.

[Price 2s. 6d.]

A REVIEW,

&c. &c.

THE House of Commons has now given its final decision with regard to the merits and demerits of Mr. Hastings. The grand inquest of England have delivered their charges, and preferred their impeachment; their allegations are referred to proof; and from the appeal to the collective wisdom and justice of the nation in the supreme tribunal of the kingdom, the question comes to be determined, whether Mr. Hastings *be guilty or not guilty?*

Whatever may be the event of the impeachment, the proper exercise of such a power is a valuable privilege of the British constitution, a formidable guardian of the public

public liberty, and the dignity of the nation. The present exercise of that popular right, coeval with the House of Commons, is without a parallel in past ages, and will be interesting to posterity. The representatives of the nation have called to their bar the supreme governor of their Indian dominions, on the supposition of delinquency; his administration, though splendid, successful, and beneficial to his country, has been charged with tyranny and oppression; overlooking his confessed and effectual services for thirteen years, which, at a critical period, saved that empire from destruction, they have preferred the vindication of the national character, to the advancement of the public interest; and erecting, in the eyes of Europe, a THRONE OF MERCY for the oppressed inhabitants of India, proceed to display their justice, and vindicate their honour, before the tribunal of the world.

Such an exertion of public virtue (if to public virtue it shall be referred) is, indeed,

Above all Greek, above all Roman fame;

and will furnish a memorable example to future times, that no station however exalted, no abilities however splendid, no services however beneficial or meritorious; that not even the smile of the sovereign, nor the voice of the people, can protect a British subject from impeachment, and a public delinquent from punishment, if found guilty.

In a question of such importance, which interests the honour of the nation, and may involve the character, the fortune, and the life of a delegated Sovereign of India, the subjects of this free government, in which all orders of men are represented in the great council of the nation, are ever ready and zealous to embrace a side. The law of Solon, which enjoined every citizen to take a part in public affairs, recommends itself forcibly to the feelings of Englishmen. The only danger is, that from the influence of faction, and the awe which is annexed to great names, they may be prompted to determine before they inquire, and to pronounce judgment

judgment without examination. But we ought to confider, that though impeachable matter has been found in the charges againſt Mr. Haſtings, nothing has been *proved*; that though he has been *accuſed* by the Houſe of Commons, he has not been *tried* by the Houſe of Peers; and that, according to the liberal principles of the law of England, he is to be *preſumed innocent till he be found guilty*. To aſſiſt the Public in the inveſtigation of this important ſubject, I ſhall preſent them with a view of the principal charges againſt the late Governor General of Bengal, eſtimate the demerit or criminality which they contain, and then adduce ſome obſervations, that may prepare the reader to form a judgment of his own.

The preamble to the articles of impeachment is the firſt thing which merits attention. The report of the Committee contains the following charge againſt Mr. Haſtings: " That, not regarding the ſacred obligation of his oath, nor the important duties of the high offices to which he

was

was appointed, but entertaining bafe and corrupt views of procuring for himfelf and his dependents exorbitant wealth, &c. he did, by many unjuftifiable acts, by him done and committed, whilft he was Prefident and Governor General of Bengal, and by various unwarrantable and criminal practices, faithlefsly, illegally, and tyrannically, violate the duties of his ftation: by each and all of which practices, the welfare of the Eaft India Company has materially fuffered, the happinefs of the native inhabitants of India been deeply affected, their confidence in Englifh faith and lenity fhaken and impaired, and the honour of the crown and character of this nation, as far as in him lay, wantonly and wickedly degraded."——Affertions fo hardy, and accufations fo atrocious, ought not to have been introduced into the preamble of an impeachment before an affembly fo refpectable as the Houfe of Peers, without the cleareft and moft uncontrovertible evidence. In all tranfactions of a political nature, there are many concealed movements, that efcape the

the detection of the world: but there are some facts so broad and glaring, so conspicuous and prominent, as to strike the general eye, and meet the common level of the human understanding. However adapted such rhetorical exaggerations might be to the character of accusers before a popular assembly, whose judgment is to be gained through the medium of the passions, they are highly improper and indecent for the Delegates of the Lower House of Parliament, when they come forward to verify assertions by proof before the highest tribunal of the kingdom; a tribunal at which the appeal is made from transient feelings and temporary passions, to the steady principles of reason, justice, and law. That the welfare of the East India Company has materially suffered by the various unwarrantable and criminal practices of Mr. Hastings, is pronounced with boldness; but where is the authority, and what is the evidence? Mercantile communities will certainly be allowed to be the best judges of their own interests. The East India Company

pany have already decided this important question. The Court of Proprietors, and the Court of Directors, have given their unanimous vote of thanks to Mr. Haftings, " for the long, faithful, and able fervices he has rendered to the Company; for having difplayed uncommon zeal, ability, and exertion, in the management of their affairs, particularly in finding refources for fupporting the war in the Carnatic, when that country was in danger of being loft, through the fuccefsful irruption of Hyder Ally Cawn, aided by the powerful affiftance of the French; and for his firm, unwearied, and fuccefsful endeavours in procuring the late peace with the feveral powers in India."

The voice of the Eaft India Company proclaims to the world, " the long, the faithful, and the meritorious fervices of Mr. Haftings;" and mankind will abide by their deliberate decifion, rather than by the intemperate affertion of a Committee, whofe patriotic fpeculations and theories of mercantile

cantile intereſt are tinged with the dark colours of impeachment and crimination.

The report of the Committee of Secrecy alſo ſtates, "That the happineſs of the native inhabitants of India has been deeply affected, their confidence in Engliſh faith and lenity ſhaken and impaired, and the character of this nation wantonly and wickedly degraded." Various complaints of a ſimilar nature have rung in the public ear concerning the miſeries of Indoſtan, and the ſufferings of the devoted inhabitants. The oppreſſed and agonizing millions of India have been repreſented as imploring the compaſſion, the juſtice, and the vengeance of this country. But where are the records of their calamities to be found? What deputies have they ſent to explain their wrongs and their ſufferings? What advocates have they appointed to petition for redreſs and relief? None. Their complaints againſt the late Governor General of Bengal have never been heard, but within the walls of the Houſe of Commons.

It

It is a fact, well known to every individual verfant in the affairs of India, that no perfon ever enjoyed the confidence both of the native and European powers, more than Mr. Haftings; that he left our Eaftern poffeffions in a tranquil and flourifhing ftate; and that his departure was attended with the moft unequivocal marks of admiration and regret from the inhabitants of Indoftan. Since the commencement of this profecution, the charges of Mr. Burke have been carried to Calcutta, and carefully circulated in India *. It was known, at that time, that Mr. Haftings had not only defcended from a public to a private ftation, but that he was perfecuted with accufations and impeachments. But none of thefe *fuffering millions* have fent their complaints to this country: not a figh nor a groan has been wafted from India to Britain. On the contrary, teftimonies the moft honourable to the character and merit of Mr. Haftings, have been tranfmitted by thofe very princes

* Mr. William Burke, a coufin of the Member of Parliament, undertook this *friendly* office.

whom he has been supposed to have loaded with the deepest injuries *. Sir John Macpherson, and Lord Cornwallis, his successors in office, have given the same voluntary tribute of approbation to his measures as Governor General of India. A letter from the former, dated the 10th of August 1786, gives the following account of our dominions in Asia: " The native inhabitants of this kingdom are the happiest and best protected subjects in India; our native allies and tributaries confide in our protection; the country powers are aspiring to the friendship of the English; and from the King of Tidore, towards New Guinea, to Timur Shaw, on the banks of the Indus, there is not a state that has not *lately* given us proofs of confidence and respect."

Does this authentic account of the administration of Mr. Hastings, and of the state of India, correspond with the gloomy picture of despotism and despair drawn by the

* Vide Major Scott's excellent speech on the charge respecting presents, p. 22. published by Stockdale.

Committee

Committee of Secrecy? Will accufations, built on fuch a bafelefs fabric, prepoffefs the Public in favour of the impeachment? What credit can we give to multiplied and accumulated charges, when we find that they originate from mifreprefentation and falfehood?

The firft article of impeachment is concerning Cheit Sing, the Zemindar of Benares. Bulwant Sing, the father of this Rajah, was merely an *Aumil*, or farmer and collector of the revenues, for Sujah ul Dowlah, Nabob of Oude, and Vizir of the Mogul empire. When, on the deceafe of his father, Cheit Sing was confirmed in the office of collector for the Vizir, he paid 200,000 pounds as a gift or nuzzeranah, and an additional rent of 30,000 pounds per annum.

As the father was no more than an *Aumil*, the fun fucceeded only to his rights and pretenfions. But by a funnud granted to him by the Nabob Sujah Dowlah in September

September 1773, through the influence of Mr. Haftings, he acquired a legal title to property in the land, and was raifed from the office of *Aumil* to the rank of Zemindar. About four years after the death of Bulwant Sing, the Governor General and Council of Bengal obtained the fovereignty paramount of the province of Benares. On the transfer of this fovereignty, the Governor and Council propofed a new grant to Cheit Sing, confirming his former privileges, and conferring upon him the addition of the fovereign rights of the mint, and the powers of criminal juftice with regard to life and death. He was then recognized by the Company as one of their Zemindars; a tributary fubject, or feudatory vaffal, of the Britifh empire in Indoftan. The feudal fyftem, which was formerly fuppofed to be peculiar to our Gothic anceftors, has always prevailed in the Eaft. In every defcription of that form of government, notwithftanding accidental variations, there are two affociations expreffed or underftood; one for internal fecurity, the other

other for external defence. The King or Nabob, confers protection on the feudatory baron as tributary prince, on condition of an annual revenue in the time of peace, and of military service, partly commutable for money, in the time of war. The feudal incidents in the middle ages in Europe, the fine paid to the superior on *marriage, wardship, relief,* &c. correspond to the annual tribute in Asia. Military service in war, and extraordinary aids in the event of extraordinary emergencies, were common to both *.

When

---

* Notwithstanding this analogy, the powers and privileges of a Zemindar have never been so well ascertained and defined as those of a Baron in the feudal ages. Though the office has usually descended to the posterity of the Zemindar, under the ceremony of fine and investiture, a material decrease in the cultivation, or decline in the population of the district, has sometimes been considered as a ground to dispossess him. When Zemindars have failed in their engagements to the state, though not to the extent to justify expulsion, supervisors have been often sent into the Zemindaries, who have farmed out the lands, and exercised authority under the Duannee laws, independent of the Zemindar. These circumstances strongly mark their *dependence* on the Nabob. About a year after the departure of Mr. Hastings from India, the question concerning

When the Governor General of Bengal in 1778, made an extraordinary demand on the Zemindar of Benares for five lacks of rupees, the British empire, in that part of the world, was surrounded with enemies which threatened its destruction. In 1779, a general confederacy was formed among the great powers of Indostan for the expulsion of the English from their Asiatic dominions. At this crisis the expectation of a French armament augmented the general calamities of the country. Mr. Hastings is charged by the Committee, with making his first demand under the false pretence that hostilities had commenced with France. Such an insidious attempt to pervert a me-

ing the rights of Zemindars was agitated at great length in Calcutta, and after the fullest and most accurate investigation, the Governor General and Council gave it as their deliberate opinion to the Court of Directors, that the property of the soil is not in the Zemindar, but in the government; and that a Zemindar is merely an officer of government appointed to collect its revenues. Cheit Sing understood himself to stand in this predicament. " I am," said he, on various occasions, " the servant of the Circar (government), and ready to obey your orders." The name and office of Zemindar is not of Hindoo, but Mogul institution.

ritorious

ritorious action into a crime, is new even in the history of impeachments. On the 7th of July 1778, Mr. Haftings received private intelligence from an English merchant at Cairo, that war had been declared by Great-Britain on the 23d of March, and by France on the 30th of April. Upon this intelligence confidered as authentic, it was determined to attack all the French fettlements in India. The information was afterwards found to be premature; but in the latter end of August, a fecret difpatch was received from England, authorifing and appointing Mr. Haftings to take the meafures which he had already adopted in the preceding month. The Directors and the Board of Controul have expreffed their approbation of this tranfaction, by liberally rewarding Mr. Baldwyn, the merchant, for fending the earlieft intelligence he could procure to Bengal. It was *two days* after Mr. Haftings's information of the French war, that he formed the refolution of exacting the five lacks of rupees from Cheit Sing, and would have made *fimilar exactions* from all the dependencies of the Company in India,

India, had they been in the fame circumftances. The fact is, that the great Zemindars of Bengal pay as much to Government as their lands can afford: Cheit Sing's collections were above fifty lacks, and his rent not twenty-four.

The right of calling for extraordinary aids and military fervice in times of danger being univerfally eftablifhed in India, as it was formerly in Europe during the feudal times, the fubfequent conduct of Mr. Haftings is explained and vindicated. The Governor General and Council of Bengal having made a demand upon a tributary Zemindar for three fucceffive years, and that demand having been refifted by their vaffal, they are juftified in his punifhment. The neceffities of the Company, in confequence of the critical fituation of their affairs in 1781, calling for a high fine; the ability of the Zemindar, who poffeffed near two crores of rupees in money and jewels, to pay the fum required; his backwardnefs to comply with the demands of his fuperiors; his difaffection to the Englifh

English interest, and desire of revolt, which even then began to appear, and were afterwards conspicuous; fully justify Mr. Hastings in every subsequent step of his conduct. In the whole of his proceedings it is manifest that he had not early formed a design hostile to the Zemindar, but was regulated by events which he could neither foresee nor controul. When the necessary measures which he had taken for supporting the authority of the Company, by punishing a refractory vassal, were thwarted and defeated by the barbarous massacre of the British troops, and the rebellion of Cheit Sing, the appeal was made to arms, an unavoidable revolution took place in Benares, and the Zemindar became the author of his own destruction.

The decision of the House of Commons on this charge against Mr. Hastings, is one of the most singular to be met with in the annals of Parliament. The Minister, who was followed by the majority, vindicated him in every thing that he had *done*, and found him blameable only for what he *intended*

intended to *do*; juftified every ftep of his *conduct*, and criminated his propofed *intention* of converting the crimes of the Zemindar to the benefit of the ftate, by a fine of fifty lacks of rupees. An impeachment of *error* in *judgment* with regard to the *quantum* of a fine, and for an *intention* that never was *executed*, and never known to the offending party, characterifes a tribunal *inquifition* rather than a Court of Parliament.

The fecond article of impeachment regards the princeffes of Oude. This queftion takes its origin from a tranfaction between the Nabob Affulph ul Dowlah and the Bhow Begum of Oude, in which, by the miniftry of Mr. Briftow, he obtained from her, in November 1775, an agreement to pay thirty lacks of rupees on the condition of the Nabob's granting to her an engagement in writing, with the Company's guarantee, that no more demands of any kind fhould ever be made upon her; and that fhe fhould enjoy, *during life*, her jaghires and other eftates and poffeffions unmolefted. The Board approved

proved of Mr. Bristow's conduct, and confirmed the guarantee. General Clavering, Colonel Monson, and Mr. Francis, formed at that time a permanent and unvaried majority in the government of Bengal; and although Mr. Hastings disapproved of that transaction, he was certainly bound to observe it by the guarantee of the council, provided no sufficient cause or necessity should arise to justify its violation*. Accordingly, in virtue of that engage-

---

* The idea entertained by Mr. Francis of the extent of the guarantee, and the rights which the Begum had acquired under it, may be known from the following circumstance: In the month of December 1775, the Begum wrote a letter to Mr. Hastings, complaining bitterly of the conduct of the Nabob, Mr. Bristow, and Murteza Cawn, the Nabob's Minister. In the same letter, she desires leave to withdraw from her son's dominions, unless Alige Cawn, Sujah Dowlah's late Minister, was re-appointed. Upon the receipt of this letter, Mr. Francis observed, that it seemed extraordinary that a lady immured in a seraglio, should presume to talk of appointing Ministers and governing kingdoms: that he believed the letter not to be of her composition, as probably she could not read, but *written by her eunuch*, who brought it to Calcutta: that he had no objection to grant the Begum an asylum in the Company's provinces, *provided the Nabob gave his consent*, without which she could have no right to remove herself, or the *immense wealth in her possession*, out of his dominions.

ment, the Begum continued in the quiet and unmolested possession of her jaghires and her treasures, till the years 1781 and 1782, when, upon the revolt and rebellion of Cheit Sing the Zemindar of Benares, the Begums of Fyzabad united their authority and influence to harass and disturb the English government in India. Circular letters were sent to the Zemindars of Oude, inciting them to rebellion; rewards were proclaimed for the heads of English officers, soldiers, and sepoys: a general revolt ensued, of which their agents were the principal leaders in the districts of Goorucpoor and Bareech; the two chief eunuchs and confidential servants of the younger Begum, openly levied troops in the great square of the city for the avowed service of Cheit Sing against the English; and these were sent, under the name of Nujubs, to Cheit Sing, and actually employed in his battles against us. These facts have been proved by the depositions of the most respectable witnesses, taken before the Chief Justice of India, with all the solemnities of law.

The

The letter of Mr. Middleton to Mr. Haſtings, dated the 17th of October 1781, contains full and complete information, ſufficient to fix this point beyond diſpute. The important facts mentioned in Mr. Middleton's letter were afterwards confirmed by the depoſitions of Colonel Hannay, Captain Williams, Captain Gordon, and Major Macdonald, as well as by the teſtimony of ſeveral native officers under their command *.

What has been oppoſed to the concurrent and univerſal voice of India, confirmed by evidence before the Houſe of Commons? Unſupported inſinuations, arbitrary conjectures, mutilated extracts from

---

* Vid. Minutes of Evidence taken before the Houſe of Commons, part iv. p. 168 *. Mr. Middleton depoſes, " It was my firm belief, that the Begums uſed every means in their power to promote the rebellion of the Rajah Cheit Sing; and that they encouraged it in the Nabob's own dominions; on that belief, for which I had *the concurrent teſtimony of the whole country*, I founded my opinion, that they had forfeited the protection of the Eaſt-India Company." The depoſition of Captain Williams, ibid. p. 163, is ſtill ſtronger and more pointed.

* Printed for Stockdale.

letters,

letters, malignant witticisms, and an accumulation of opprobrious epithets and personal abuse, unworthy of a grave assembly, and insulting to the dignity of Parliament. Did it ever happen in a court of law, in any civilized country, that circumstantial and constructive evidence was preferred to direct and positive proof? In the absence of the latter, the former is often admitted; but he would be a strange judge indeed, who should believe his own conjectures and constructions in opposition to direct and positive proof! The character of the Begum, who, according to Mr. Francis, presumed, on former occasions, " to talk of appointing ministers and governing kingdoms," gives credibility to the charges against her; the evidence produced was sufficient to convince the Governor General of her treacherous and hostile intentions: with justice, therefore, as well as wisdom, he gave orders to seize those treasures, which put the city at her devotion, and to resume those jaghires (giving at the same time an equivalent,) which enabled her

her to keep up numerous bands of military attendants *.

If the behaviour of the Begums, who had formerly abetted the rebellion of Cheit Sing, and were then in a state of revolt,

---

* The only objectionable part of Mr. Hastings's conduct throughout this business appears to have been his consenting to take affidavits in order to prove a fact of universal notoriety: his motive, however, he has explained in the Benares Narrative. It was not to satisfy himself, but to convince others, that the revolt of Cheit Sing (though not the moment of revolt) was premeditated. I mean not to anticipate the additional evidence which is now in England, both with respect to the Begums and Cheit Sing: it is impossible, however, to pass over one very remarkable fact. In the original charges, reflections were cast upon Colonel Hannay and Captain Gordon for omitting to state, in their affidavits, the letters of civility which passed between them and the Begum. Colonel Hannay was dead; but Captain Gordon, the brother of Lieutenant Colonel Gordon, was then in England, and might have been summoned to state the fact. Mr. Burke did not call him in 1786, and Mr. Hastings would call no person. In Mr. Sheridan's speech * the next year, he laid particular stress on this circumstance. Captain Gordon, who was in the south of France at the time, came over to England immediately on reading Mr. Sheridan's speech, but too late to defend himself before the House of Commons. Of course he reserves himself for another tribunal,

* Printed for Stockdale.

justified the proceedings of the English government against them, the situation of our affairs in the East rendered them not only expedient but necessary. In every form of government, even the most free, a discretionary and despotic power must sometimes be exercised. There are critical periods in human affairs, when a strict conformity to the letter of the law may endanger the safety of the nation and the existence of the state. In such situations it is given in charge to the supreme executive power, " *Ne quid detrimenti respublica capiat.*" Political necessity, like self-preservation, supersedes all laws. The certainty of danger will excuse the exertion, and the public safety justify the infringement. Pusillanimity at such a period is tacit treason against the state, which enjoins us to prefer the security of the public to that of the individual. Then the laws of all nations, like those of Sparta, after the battle of Leuctra, " sleep for one moment, that they may awake for ever."

The situation of India, at the period when Mr. Hastings supported the Nabob of Oude, in seizing the treasures, and resuming the jaghires of the Begum, was one of the most critical and momentous to be found, even in a history so full of sudden revolutions and unexpected catastrophes as that of Indostan. In September 1780, intelligence was received in Calcutta, that Hyder Ally Cawn had defeated the British troops commanded by Colonel Baillie, and that Sir Hector Monro had found it necessary to retreat to Madras. At the same time, accounts arrived, that a strong armament was expected from the island of Mauritius, in order to co-operate with Hyder Ally. When Sir Eyre Coote arrived in safety at Madras *, with a reinforcement of men, money, and provisions, he wrote to the Governor and Council, that his army must in future be paid and fed from Bengal; and that with every assistance that could be given him the issue would be exceedingly doubtful. At this moment Chim-

* The 4th of November 1780.

nagee Boosla, the son of Moodagee, was at the head of an army of Mahrattas at Cuttack, which had marched for the avowed purpose of invading Bengal. This impending storm Mr. Hastings averted, by the payment of sixteen lacks of rupees, and withdrew Moodagee from the confederacy. He secured the unmolested march of Colonel Pearce, at the head of ten battalions of Sepoys, to join Sir Eyre Coote, before the second action with Hyder; and he effectually broke the combination that was formed against the English interest in India; a service once condemned by a vote of the House of Commons, but which is now approved and applauded by every enlightened man, who is acquainted with the state of our affairs in the East. All the money that could be procured upon bond was borrowed, previous to the departure of Mr. Hastings from Calcutta, in July 1781, when he proceeded to Benares. The funds of the Company were exhausted, but the public necessities daily encreased. Even the opposers of Mr. Hastings have allowed, that to his spirited exertions

tions at that time, we are indebted for the preservation of the Carnatic. Mr. Dundas has formerly declared, " that he could not comprehend how Mr. Haſtings contrived to raiſe money, but that he had done ſo; and that without money our empire in India would have been loſt."

One remarkable circumſtance proves the diſtreſs to which the Engliſh Adminiſtration was then reduced. The army in Bengal was conſiderably in arrears. The inveſtment of the Company was ſupported by loans; and, in November 1781, when it was abſolutely neceſſary to ſend conſiderable ſupplies of money to Sir Eyre Coote, the Council at Calcutta could not complete the ſum from the public treaſury, but obtained it on the credit of a principal native in Calcutta. The army in Oude, the brigade at Cawnpore, Colonel Muir's army in the country of the Mahrattas, were in arrears and mutinous: vaſt ſums were required at Madras and Bombay. Mr. Haſtings knew that Suffrein would appear on the

Coaſt

Coaft early in 1782; and without the moft ftrenuous exertions, India would have been loft to this empire. The fifty-five lacks of rupees feized from the rebellious Begums, warranted by the ftricteft juftice, and fanctioned by the ftrongeft neceffity, were no where elfe to be found: and without fuch a feafonable fupply, Mr. Haftings might now have been in the fituation of thofe commanders, who, after having difmembered the Britifh dominions, fought a refuge from minifterial impeachment, and the vengeance of their country, under the all-atoning robe of Patriotifm, and in the all-protecting fanctuary of Oppofition. To underftand our affairs in India, we muft seek for a parallel, not in modern, but in ancient hiftory, when a conquering army was fupplied by the cities and provinces through which it marched. In that quarter of the globe we cannot borrow millions, upon the ftrength of taxes, which throw a burden on remoteft pofterity. Our dominions in India muft be preferved by the extended arm; danger muft be repelled,

and

and destruction averted, by the exertions of the moment; and he who starts at accusation, or shrinks from responsibility, will lose a distance province. There are seasons in which every eastern conqueror, like Alexander the Great, must cut the Gordian knot with the sword; and when the duration of empire depends on the hour, it may be lawful, and even meritorious, to invade a Zenana or plunder a Mosque *.

It

---

* It has been repeatedly said, that Mr. Hastings vindicated his conduct on improper grounds, and that if he had rested his defence on state necessity, he would have been fully justified. The necessity has been proved beyond the possibility of contradiction. A hundred thousand men, scattered through every part of India, all five months in arrears, depended upon Bengal for present and future supply. Suffrein and a French army were on the point of arriving. The Bengal treasury was exhausted, and every mode of raising money at an end. What revenues were there, but a fine to be levied on Cheit Sing for his rebellion, and the recovery of the Nabob's debt to the Company? Mr. Hastings failed in the first; but between the 20th of January, and the 10th of September, 1782, one hundred and twenty-eight lacks of rupees were received from the Nabob. This, and the improvement of the revenue of Bengal, were the funds which, as Sir John Macpherson truly stated, carried us through the war, and preserved India to Great Britain. I am not

advancing

It is impossible to dismiss this article without remarking the ignorance or disingenuity which distinguished both parties in the House of Commons in their deliberations on this question. The discord between the Nabob of Oude and the Begum, unjustly ascribed to Mr. Hastings, has been represented as a peculiar and unparalleled enormity; as if similar quarrels from opposite interests were not common, and almost universal in the East. We find in the history of the Ottoman empire, the Valid Sultaness, or mother of the Sultan, perpetually attempting to direct or to disturb the government of her son *; and these domestic dissensions and intrigues are the principal causes of the revolutions which take place in the seraglio. The annals of Indostan, and particularly of Oude, furnish

advancing new assertions; at the time when the existence of the necessity was disputed in the House of Commons, their table was covered with documents, containing much stronger proofs than I have now collected.

* Mignot's Hist. Ottom. Emp.

us

us with the same opposition of interests and jealousy of power. The unbounded ambition of the Begum is mentioned by the accusers of Mr. Hastings, and it is very properly stated in the article of impeachment, " that the Nabob attempted, on former occasions, to seize the treasures of his mother."

The distresses of the women in the Khord Mahal, and the sufferings of the eunuchs, or confidential servants of the Begum, have been magnified beyond measure, and decked in the dismal colours of pathetic eloquence, as if the gloomy imagination of a poet was furnishing a scene in tragedy. But the apartment of the women is concealed from European eyes, and its transactions unknown. The severities inflicted on the eunuchs, and the distresses of the women, so far from originating with Mr. Hastings, were never communicated to him till after the release of the latter and the relief of the former.

One material circumstance, with regard to this transaction, ought not to be forgotten. When the Court of Directors sent an order to enquire into the guilt or innocence of the Begum during the period of Cheit Sing's rebellion, the majority of the Council was adverse to the Governor General. Mr. Wheler expressed his conviction, from the evidence of impartial witnesses, that the Begums had been concerned in the rebellion, but proposed that an inquiry should be made, which was seconded by Mr. Stables. Mr. Hastings represented it as unnecessary, as no complaint had ever been made by the Begums; but added, that if an inquiry was to be made, it should be from all persons capable of giving information. Mr. Macpherson also opposed the inquiry, and professed his belief in the rebellion of the Begums. The Council, though united against Mr. Hastings, dropped the inquiry. According to their construction of the letter from the Court of Directors, no order was given to authorize a legal inquiry into that affair; and

and it is plain, that their construction was well founded, since neither the Court of Directors, nor the Board of Controul, have resumed the subject from February 1783, to the present day. But they have given a decision of more importance. They have added their SOLEMN SANCTION to *all the proceedings of Mr. Hastings in Oude*; and have given positive orders, that his *final arrangement* with the Nabob Vizir shall have the *force* and *authority* of *law*.

The next article of impeachment, of any importance, is contracts and salaries. It will not admit of a dispute, that it was the duty of the Governor General of Bengal to attend strictly to the expenditure of the public money; and, more particularly in a time of war and public distress, to be careful that those revenues, upon which the welfare and safety of the empire did necessarily depend, should not be diminished by dissipation or prodigality, and should not be diverted from the public service, or squandered for the purpose of increasing a corrupt

corrupt perſonal influence, or providing for venal dependants. Nor is it denied, that in the inſtructions given by the Court of Directors to the Governor General and Council, 1774, it is ſpecially directed, that all contracts, with the conditions, ſhould be publicly advertiſed, and ſealed propoſals delivered in for the ſame; and that every propoſal ſhould be opened in Council, and the preference given to the loweſt, provided ſufficient ſecurity ſhould be offered for the performance of the ſame. All general regulations, however, admit of particular exceptions, in which they are " more honoured in the breach than in the obſervance;" and in which the ſpirit of the law may be preſerved, though its forms are neglected. Mr. Haſtings in his defence has fairly and honourably avowed this principle. " According to my conſtruction of the Company's orders, they never were nor could be meant, in any inſtance, to leave their adminiſtration in India without an option: at ſuch a diſtance from the parent ſtate, the government on the ſpot muſt be veſted

vested with a discretionary power." This power of interpreting general laws, and judging of their particular application, must necessarily belong to every Governor of distant provinces, more particularly of India, where the sentiments and manners of the inhabitants are so different from ours, and where politics are perpetually fluctuating, and interests continually changing. A liberal construction is there to be given to orders and instructions, and a latitude allowed to those who carry them into execution, in order to accommodate them to accidental circumstances, and the varying situations of the moment. Were this power not permitted, the most pernicious consequences might take place from a blind observance of positive instructions, framed by persons ignorant of the real state of the country, and calculated for occasions that no longer existed.

Let us examine the contracts that have been most complained of. Some of them, such

such as the marine contract, and that for embanking the river of Chittigong, are so trifling and insignificant, as not to involve the smallest censure, much less to compose a charge for an impeachment; and they were even rejected by the party who proposed them. Others are in the highest degree honourable to Mr. Hastings, and throw a lustre on his administration. Of this number was the contract for supplying Fort William with the necessary stores and provisions in the event of a siege. Fort William was of as much importance in Asia, as Gibraltar in Europe; and the very place in India, which, from its situation and uncommon value, was the most liable to an attack from an enemy.

In the same respectable class is Mr. Auriol's contract for supplying the settlements on the Carnatic; and instead of being an object of censure, much less of impeachment, reflects signal honour on the wisdom and public spirit of Mr. Hastings.

When Madras and its dependencies were in imminent danger of being deſtroyed by famine, the Governor of Bengal, with a promptitude and an energy which were of the moſt beneficial conſequence to all our poſſeſſions in India, determined upon their immediate relief. At the moment when the very exiſtence of the Carnatic was at ſtake, when the lives of his countrymen, and the Britiſh dominions in India, depended on his ſpirit and diſpatch, was he to follow the frigid line of official conduct, and delay ſending the means of preſervation, until he ſhould diſcover the cheapeſt method by which thoſe means were to be procured? Was he to proclaim to the enemies of Great-Britain, that a moſt valuable part of our territory was likely to be a prey to famine, and to point out the method of intercepting the means which he was about to ſend to their relief? No. The nature of the caſe impoſed on him the neceſſity of exceeding the orders of the Company, and to have heſitated about diſobedience, would have been highly criminal. Arduous ſituations

tions of this kind distinguish the man of genius from the mere official character, and mark the spirited patriot, who can serve his country in cases of danger, from the time-serving politician, who entrenches himself in forms, and shelters his pusillanimity under the letter of the law *.

With regard to the opium contract, no alterations had been made by Mr. Hastings.

* Let me here do justice to the candour of Mr. Pitt.—He spoke of Mr. Hastings's conduct, in thus preserving a nation from famine, with all the enthusiasm which such a conduct deserved. Nor did he stop here. He gave Mr. Auriol the praise which was his due; he observed, that the fortune earned by so meritorious a service, however large it might be, was honourably acquired; and that Mr. Auriol had shewn himself worthy of the confidence which Mr. Hastings had placed in him. Nor was this all: Mr. Pitt, after having proved the importance of the service performed, defended the plan as the most œconomical that could have been adopted. But what shall we say of the Government of Madras, who could meanly and basely complain to the Court of Directors of the terms of this agency, while they were almost hourly writing to Bengal—" Send us rice upon every ship, and at any expence, or we perish.—Thanks for your great and liberal supplies of money and provisions; but unless both are continued to the utmost possible extent, we are undone."

Opium

Opium was a monopoly in India during the Mahomedan government, and given to favoured individuals. From the time that the English acquired influence in that country, it was a monopoly in the hands of the Company at Patna; openly and avowedly taken as a perquisite of office; perfectly known to the Government of Bengal, and the Court of Directors in London. Mr. Hastings, on his accession to the Government in 1772, first made the Company partakers in this monopoly, and created a revenue for them; not in consequence of orders from England, but from the motions of a mind that watched for the interests of his constituents. That this contract, like that with regard to elephants and bullocks, was beneficial to individuals, necessarily results from the established maxims and conduct of mankind. Is there any person so ignorant of the principles of political society, or who has considered the contracts given in the late German war, or in the American war, who can construe into a crime the conduct of the late Governor General

General of Bengal, in difpofing of laborious and lucrative offices, in fuch a manner as would at once benefit the India Company, and attach individuals to its fervice? The conduct of all adminiftrations, in all nations and ages of the world, would be a fatire on the fuppofition. But although this article of impeachment had been as injurious to the character of Mr. Haftings, as it is evidently favourable, it can no longer be the fubject of public deliberation. After the contracts firft attracted the confideration of the Directors, they became the objects of parliamentary inquiry. The refult was favourable to Mr. Haftings; for, fubfequent to that inquiry and inveftigation, he was repeatedly appointed by Parliament to his high and confidential fituation in India. If Parliament, after having examined the grounds of the charge, and, in confequence of that examination, had re-appointed Mr. Haftings to his former ftation; with what propriety, decency, or common fenfe, can they, at a fubfequent period, without new evidence

against

against him, convert those charges into articles of impeachment, which formerly they had not considered as a disqualification to the renewal of a high and important trust? An absurdity so glaring must strike every person, who is free from prejudice, and acquainted with the forms of law. In this article, the severest moralist will find no ground for a criminal charge, except against the honourable gentlemen who have brought it forwards.

In the war before the last, this nation added seventy millions to her public debt: in that war one man acquired by one contract six hundred thousand pounds; and Lord Holland and his confidential clerks, at least one million sterling. In the late war, a hundred millions were added to the public debt; and the extravagance of the treasury contracts was a theme for almost the daily declamation of Mr. Fox and Mr. Burke. After a severe review of the expenditure of public money, during Mr. Hastings' administration of thirteen years, four contracts

tracts have been deemed objectionable, two of them the minister defended as highly praise-worthy, the third resulted from a productive revenue, created by Mr. Hastings himself; the fourth, the bullock contract, was proposed by the Commander in Chief, and was approved by every officer in the army.

The sixth article of impeachment relates to presents received by Mr. Hastings. Among nations in the infancy of society, no business is carried on, and no transaction concluded, without gifts and presents. This custom prevailed universally among the nations of America when it was first discovered, and is ascribed by Tacitus to the ancient Germans: " Muneribus gaudent, sed nec data imputant, nec acceptis obligantur." But in a more advanced state of society among the German tribes, what was formerly considered as the confirmation of a bargain, or the seal of a treaty, became a matter of obligation. The voluntary donations from the attendants to the

the Chief, at firſt expreſſions of affection, or acknowledgments of gratitude, were eſtabliſhed into permanent uſages; and hence aroſe the feudal incidents in the middle ages. The Aſiatic nations, who have preſerved ſo many of the original cuſtoms of mankind, have always retained this. It forms a ceremonial of intercourſe between inferiors and ſuperiors; and no tranſaction is carried on or concluded that is not accompanied with a preſent. So much does this enter into general practice and common life, that " to approach a king or great man with gifts*," forms a part of the inſpired code of Oriental morality. What in Europe would be conſidered as receiving a bribe, is no more in India than complying with an eſtabliſhed cuſtom, and the uniform practice of the country. But as, during Lord Clive's adminiſtration, this cuſtom had been abuſed, and the princes of India oppreſſed by the rapacity and extortions of ſome ſervants of the

* Solom. Proverbs.

Company,

Company, an Act of Parliament to regulate the acceptance of presents was passed in 1773. It was then enacted, "That no Governor General, nor any of the Council, shall directly, for his or their use, or on his or their behalf, accept, receive, or take from any person or persons, on any account whatsoever, any gift, gratuity, donation, or reward;—and it is hereby further enacted, that every such present, gift, gratuity, or reward, accepted, taken, or received, shall be deemed and construed to have been received and taken to and for the sole use of the said United Company."

The natural and obvious construction of these words is, that the Governor General and Council were prohibited from accepting presents on their own account, but not on that of the Company. And this was the construction which was put upon it by Mr. Hastings, by the Court of Directors, and the Board of Controul. On various occasions Mr. Hastings informed the Directors, that he had received presents

for

for the benefit of the Company; and in their anfwers no hint is expreffed that the act was illegal. On one occafion, on the receipt of a prefent from the Nabob Vizir in September 1781, which was expended upon, as received in, the public fervice, Mr. Haftings communicated it to the Court of Directors in January 1782, defiring their permiffion to appropriate it to his own ufe. The anfwer of the Directors fully explains their fentiments on this fubject. It ftates that however favourable their inclinations might be to Mr. Haftings, they could not comply with his requeft, as he was precluded by law from accepting prefents; and they proceed to mention that, by the fame law, all prefents received in India are deemed to be taken for the *fole ufe of the Company:* this letter had the fanction of the Treafury, when Mr. Pitt, the prefent Minifter, was Chancellor of the Exchequer. If there be any meaning in language, if words can convey ideas, the obvious interpretation of thefe letters is, that though the Governor General could not accept of prefents on his *own account*, he might

might receive them for the *benefit of his constituents*.

But the strongest confirmation that this was the genuine sense of the regulating Act 1773, is Mr. Pitt's Bill 1784*, in which there is a particular clause prohibiting the acceptance of presents, " for the use of the party receiving the same, or for, or pretended to be for, the use of the said Company." This proves, beyond the possibility of a doubt, that the old law was incomplete, and hence the new clause in the Bill 1784 extending the regulation to the Company as well as its servants. By the forty-seventh clause of the same bill it is ordained, " that so much of the Act 1773, as subjects any person receiving gifts or presents, to any penalty or forfeiture for so doing, or *as directs that such gifts and presents shall belong to the said Company, shall be repealed*, from and after the first of January 1785; provided that no prosecutions or other suits, already com-

---

* Printed for Stockdale; with Observations.

menced

menced or to be commenced, *before the first of January 1785, upon the said Act*, shall be affected by the repeal." If both Houses of Parliament had deliberated for ages, they could not have expressed more strongly their assent to the construction put on the Act 1773 by Mr. Hastings, the Court of Directors, and the Board of Controul.

Such being the interpretation of the regulating Act 1773, no criminal charge can be brought against Mr. Hastings with regard to this article, as he made no infringement on the law. He accepted the presents offered to him from no mercenary or corrupt motive; he reaped no emolument from the money which was presented; every rupee he received was paid into the treasury of the India Company, and applied to the public service. Indeed, avarice and private rapacity have never been imputed to him by his personal enemies.

Mr. Hastings is open, and justly so, to the strictest investigation of his conduct with respect to the men from whom he received presents. If it can be proved that he favoured any one of them at the public expence; that he gratified them by lucrative appointments, or entered into corrupt jobs with them, then his plea of accepting the money for the Company's use cannot avail him: but no man has attempted to prove, that Mr. Hastings was not anxious to raise the greatest possible revenue from Burdwan, Nuddea, Dingepore, and Bahar; and he is impeached for procuring the payment of the Nabob Vizir's debt to the Company, by encouraging him to perform an act of rigour and severity.

The next article (Revenues) was rejected by Mr. Pitt, but carried in a Committee by a majority of fifteen. The House has since rejected Mr. Francis who brought it forward: it proceeds upon a question as to to the rights of Zemindars; upon which no man in England can be competent to decide. Mr. Haftings had the Company's orders to let the lands of Bengal to farm; he did fo; the Directors approved it; and the fame mode is purfued, with few exceptions, to the prefent hour.

Thefe are the principal charges againft Mr. Haftings; and on thefe his accufers reft the fuccefs of the impeachment. Ingenious fophifty may pervert the plaineft facts; eloquence can tincture innocence with the colours of guilt: but the intelligent and informed reader, who can difcover in thefe charges, when fcrutinized, the traces of criminality that have been afcribed to them, muft poffefs a mind more difpofed to crimination than to candour, more influenced by prejudice than acceffible to reafon.

The other charges are fo infignificant in themfelves, or founded on fuch grofs mifreprefentations, that they would not affect an obscure individual, much less a public character. They are merely added to swell the catalogue of accusations, as if the boldness of calumny could ensure its success, and a multiplicity of charges were an accumulation of crimes *. Thirteen of them passed in the House of Commons not only without investigation, but without being read; and the votes were given without enquiry, argument, or conviction. A majority had determined to impeach; opposite parties met each other, and "justled in the dark," to perplex the political drama, and bring the hero to a tragic catastrophe.

The authentic statement of facts which has been given, and the arguments which

* Human nature, at least in its dark sides, is always the same. In the last century, when Episcopacy was abolished in Scotland, a paper was read in all the churches of the kingdom, containing an accusation against the Bishops, " as guilty, all of them, of heresy, simony, bribery, perjury, cheating, incest, adultery, fornication, common swearing, drunkenness, gaming, breach of the Sabbath, and every other crime that had occurred to the accusers." Hume's Hist. vol. vi. p. 334.

have

have been employed, are, I think, sufficient to vindicate the character and conduct of Mr. Hastings, even on the maxims of European policy. When he was appointed Governor General of Bengal, he was invested with a discretionary power to promote the interests of the India Company, and of the British empire in that quarter of the globe. The general instructions sent to him from his constituents were, " That in all your deliberations and resolutions, you make the safety and prosperity of Bengal your principal object, and fix your attention on the security of the possessions and revenues of the Company." His superior genius sometimes acted in the spirit, rather than complied with the letter, of the law; but he discharged the trust, and preserved the empire committed to his care, in the same way, and with greater splendor and success than any of his predecessors in office: his departure from India was marked with the lamentations of the natives and the gratitude of his countrymen; and on his return to England, he received the

the cordial congratulations of that numerous and respectable society, whose interests he had promoted, and whose dominions he had protected and extended.

But in order to estimate aright the merits or defects of any administration, we ought to consider the scene of its operations, and the character of the people who are governed. The diversities of human nature, the varieties among mankind, are as remarkable and striking, as those of the globe which they inhabit. The climate of Indostan is not more different from that of England, than the maxims of policy established in Asia are from those which have prevailed in Europe. The actual institutions which prevailed at Athens, Sparta, and Rome, on the supposition of their revival in modern times, would be considered as Platonic visions or Utopian projects. Although the essence of public and private virtue be every where the same, the forms and expressions are every where different: the Lacedemonian government, so much cele-

celebrated in antiquity, would be considered at present as a paradox in politics; and the perfect character of the Greeks, as has been shewn by an ingenious philosopher*, would be execrated in France or England.

From the earliest records of time, the political code of Asia hath always differed essentially from the political code of Europe. The kingdoms of the East, though feudal in their form, have been always despotic in their nature. Examine the volumes of history; survey the annals of Asia for three thousand years past; you find one form of government invariably to prevail; absolute authority universally established. " The power of the King is every thing, the rights of the people nothing;" is the description which Montesquieu gives of the Oriental empires; is the maxim which Tamerlane lays down in his laws; and which, antecedent to both, Nature has established in that division of the world.

* Hume's Treatise on Morals.

Who

Who dare say to the king what dost thou? characterises Asia, from the subjects of the great Monarch of Persia, to those of the petty Rajah of Jerusalem, and from the ancient æra of Ninus, to the recent reign of Hyder Ally. At thirteen different periods hath Asia been over-run and subdued by the nations of the West or of the North; still, however, amidst all its changes, the predominant features have been the same. The conquerors assumed at once the manners of the conquered people; a revolution effected only the alteration of a name in the reigning family: the Sovereign was changed, but the Despot remained. The rude Scythian, who had no sceptre but his sword, and no palace but his tent, erected the throne of despotism; and wandering hords, accustomed to the wild freedom of nature, submitted to the yoke of servitude. The Grecian patriotism gave way to the predominating spirit of the East; and the Hero of Macedon, who had fought and conquered among his equals, became a tyrant over slaves. The Hebrew tribes,

after

after their long wanderings in the deserts of Arabia, when they settled in Palestine, rejected the authority of God himself, and required to be governed by a Despot, like the nations around them *. Among the people of the East, these political propensities have become blended with human nature; and they cannot so much as conceive the idea of another form of government †.

We have now the experience of ages to demonstrate, that any attempts to introduce European maxims and manners among the Asiatic nations, must be for ever in vain. Nature, and long-established habits stronger than nature, fix unsurmountable

* 1 Sam. iii. 19, 20.

† Mr. Gibbon, in the first volume of his History of the Decline and Fall of the Roman Empire, after mentioning the prevalence of despotism in the East in all ages, adds, " The English of late have endeavoured to communicate to the inhabitants of India ideas of a more liberal form of government; they could not have done them a more essential injury." The calm voice of philosophy in the closet certainly merits attention.

obstacles in the way. IMMUTABILITY appears to be the characteristic of Asia, and its forms, like the laws of the Medes and Persians, are incapable of change. The manners of the Persians and Indians of this day originate from the same spirit, and exhibit the same appearance, that prevailed among their ancestors at a period too remote for historical research. With an astonishing attachment to their own usages and customs, they have an inveterate and invincible aversion to those of the Europeans. Asia and Europe have been in contact for three thousand years; and although many innovations and improvements have passed from the former to the latter, not a single trace can be found of one custom, originally European, having been adopted by the nations of Asia. Even the Turks, notwithstanding their vicinity to Europe, and their intercourse with the most enlightened and refined nations of our Continent, preserve the Oriental character pure and unchanged, as if they had been separated from us by

the

the mountains of Thibet, or the rivers Ganges and Burrampooter *.

When the Britiſh power was eſtabliſhed in Indoſtan, it ſucceeded to all the rights and privileges of the Mogul empire, on the ruins of which it aroſe. The Engliſh, at their firſt ſettlement in India, were merely mercantile adventurers, and carried on a trade with the natives in the ſame manner as they do with the Chineſe. Our dominions there, like the progreſs of empire in moſt parts of the world, aroſe not from a preconceived plan of ambition, but from an accidental combination of circumſtances, which neceſſity, and that natural providence which belongs to ſocieties as well as individuals, directed and improved ſo as to blend territorial dominion with commercial advantages. The invaſion of

* The origin of deſpotiſm in Aſia, and the cauſes of its uniform appearance and permanent exiſtence in that part of the world, the reader may find illuſtrated with much ingenuity and eloquence, in a *Diſſertation on the Government, Manners, and Spirit of Aſia*, lately publiſhed by Mr. Logan.

Nadir Shah nearly accomplished the destruction of the Mogul empire, which had been gradually declining since the death of Aurengzebe. The forms of government were preserved, but the spring of authority was lost. Ally Verdy Cawn, Nabob of Bengal in 1740, usurped the sovereign power after he had murdered his predecessor, and transmitted the government, though in opposition to the laws of the empire, to his grandson Surajah Dowlah. In 1756, that inhuman tyrant wantonly attacked the English, who, from their first settlement in Bengal, had carried on their commercial pursuits in tranquillity, without forming any plans of ambition or policy to disturb the established government. In consequence of this attack the English were driven from their forts and settlements, and many of them were put to the sword. After various adventures, by their singular and vigorous exertions, they not only recovered their former footing in Bengal, but effected a revolution in the country,

country, and laid the foundation of the British empire in Indoſtan.

In the firſt effuſions of youthful patriotiſm, it is natural to wiſh, that wherever the Britiſh ſtandard is planted, it ſhould conſecrate the ſoil to Liberty, and to what, for a century paſt, we have deemed the rights of mankind. But a large and liberal acquaintance with the hiſtory of our ſpecies, will teach us, that freedom is a boon which cannot be conferred, and that it muſt ſpring from the patriotic feelings and active exertions of the people. To govern conquered provinces according to their ancient laws and eſtabliſhed cuſtoms, has been the wiſe and beneficent policy of all civilized nations. No puniſhment could be ſo ſevere to the natives of India as to ſubmit to the laws of England. The genius of Britiſh freedom would to them be a demon of terror. Political prejudices, derived from an unknown antiquity, ſtrengthened in the courſe of thouſands of years, and confirmed by the ſolemn ſanctions of religion,

religion, would make them revolt at the idea; and they would confider it as impiety, as well as rebellion, to renounce the habits of immemorial time, and the cuftoms of their fathers. The confinement and flavery of the women, refulting from the inexorable law of neceffity, in a torrid clime, might furnifh an ample fubject for declamation in the Houfe of Commons, and fuperadd many an elegant and pathetic period to the orations of a Burke and a Sheridan. The *faireft part of the fair creation*, fecluded from fociety, guarded by eunuchs, and trembling at the nod of a mafter, till the concealment of their forrows and their wifhes, " like a worm in the bud, preys on their damafk cheeks," would furely intereft the feelings of every Britifh bofom. The fighs of neglected beauty, the pangs of defpifed love, tears of tendernefs fhed in the folitude of the Haram, or the Khord Mahal, could not fail to awake fympathetic emotions in St. Stephen's Chapel; till the Members *faw*, or *thought they faw*, the formerly invifible *millions of*
diftreffed

distressed damsels stretching out their hands, and imploring relief; and *heard*, or *thought they heard*, the congratulations of their gratitude re-echoed from the *blue vault* of heaven, and wafted on the *downy pinions of the zephyr*, to the *tender texture* of their *sentimental bosoms!*

If, in alluding to a speech which intermixed tragedy with farce, I have in some measure caught the contagion, I hope I shall be forgiven. The mind, when raised to a high tone, may be allowed occasionally to relax; nor is it forbidden by the wisest of men, to answer a certain description of orators according to their own arguments.

An innovation in this grand arrangement of domestic life, however conformable to European manners, would unhinge the government, strangle the happiness, and send a poignard to the heart of India.

This is only one trait of the picture; all the other features correspond. The introduction of English maxims, manners, and laws into India, would be the severest calamity which the natives have ever experienced from the Government of Britain. If we assume a dominion over a people whose modes of thinking, and habits of acting, are so different from our own, that dominion is to be maintained by adapting our administration to their apprehensions and feelings, and not vainly attempting to subjugate their minds to the novelty of our ideas. The estimate of the merits or demerits of any administration must be formed on the scene of its influence and operations. Merit of every kind must be tried by a contiguous and cotemporary standard. Transactions at Fyzabad or Furruckabad, Oude, or Benares, are reviewed by ignorance and apathy on the banks of the Thames. The maxims of one country apply not to another. Shakespeare is not to be judged by Aristotle's rules; nor Aristotle's philosophy by the Novum Organum of Lord Bacon;

nor

nor the victorious disciple of Aristotle by the common law of England. An Asiatic empire would soon moulder away, unless it were preserved by the extended arm. An Indian sceptre would become a bauble unless it were supported by the sword. So sensible at last have the English administration become of this important truth, that, though they have censured Mr. Hastings for stepping beyond the line of official orders, when prompted by necessity and duty, they have invested the present Governor of Bengal with greater powers, and, by uniting the offices of Governor General and Commander in Chief, have appointed him in some measure Dictator of India.

2. In reviewing the administration of a Governor General of Bengal, we ought not only to consider the original and eternal forms of government established by nature in the regions of Asia, but to examine the particular map of India, and contemplate the character of the native Princes,

Princes, Nabobs, Soubahs, and Rajahs, with whom he had to act. A free and regular government, founded on principles of equity, and afcertained by laws, is the greateſt improvement which the human genius, aided by the experience of ages, has introduced into ſome favoured corners of the world. The natural and neceſſary confequences refulting from defpotifm, explain the progrefs, though they do not vindicate the character, of that defective and corrupted policy which has ever prevailed in the Eaſt. When authority is not founded on law, but on fuperior force, there will be cruelty and oppreſſion on the part of the governors, diſſimulation and ſtratagem on the part of the governed. Hence the ancient as well as modern hiſtory of the Eaſt, is almoſt a continued ſcene of crimes and calamities, of bloodſhed and horror.

The records of the kingdoms of Judah and Iſrael, a portion of Aſiatic hiſtory known to every reader, illuſtrate the ſpirit and maxims of Oriental rule. A defpotic throne,

throne, founded on the fears of the subjects, but liable to be shaken by conspiracy; rapid revolutions, effected by the sword; intrigues and plots among the descendants of the royal family for the succession to the crown; the revolt of a favourite or a general to supplant his master, and wrest the sceptre from his hand; insecurity to the lives and property of the subjects, who pass with facility and tameness, from the yoke of one tyrant to that of another; constitute the uniform and calamitous history of these petty kingdoms. Although the arts of luxury and refinement have been known in the East from the earliest times, their maxims of war and policy are scarcely superior to those of the barbarous and vagabond tribes of Scythia, by whom they have been so often subdued. They acknowledge no rights but those of the sword, and have not conceived the idea of a law of nations. They break leagues, and violate engagements, when it is no longer convenient to keep them: and engage in wars, whenever they are sufficiently powerful to take the field. Hence their political maxims are so different from ours. Power justifies oppression; humanity is deemed weakness; fraud, cunning, and treachery, become the legitimate weapons of the feeble against the violence of the strong. In the Jewish records, we find one king * dethroned, and another † doomed to destruction, for what, according to our ideas, were acts of compassion and clemency; but that generosity which, among a people truly refined, converts an enemy into a friend, among nations whose manners are barbarous, is warming a frozen snake to sting the bosom by which it is cherished. Eradut Khan, in his Memoirs, relating that Jehaun Shaw had spared the life of an enemy, makes the following reflection: " Though Jehaun Shaw was generous in this action, yet the policy of Government will not admit of such conduct being copied as an example of propriety. The world is *deceitful*, and cannot be commanded but by

---

* Saul, for sparing the life of Agag.
† Ahab, for sparing the king of Samaria.

deceit.

deceit. The thief who should wake his sleeping prey, would only bring ruin on his own head *." These facts exhibit a system of manners very different from ours, and shew, that in Asia the theory of morals agrees with the practice.

Independent of the general character of Oriental government, the course of history for half a century past, has presented the political map of India in its darkest lines and most odious colours. The most favourable aspect of the eastern monarchies, is that of a great empire, extending its authority over many dependent provinces. Such was the empire of Cyrus, the most extensive and renowned of antiquity; such would have been the empire of Alexander, who had talents to govern, as well as to subdue the world, had fate permitted him to enjoy a longer life. Absolute power, when spread over a wide circumference, is more salutary to the subjects, than when split into separate sections: the authority of

* Mem. Erad. Khan, p. 74. Printed for Stockdale.

one despot is milder and more beneficent than the tyranny of twenty. History remarks the difference between the empire of Alexander and that of his successors.

Upon the invasion of Indostan by Shaw Nadir, the Mogul Empire was dismembered, and divided into fragments. The tributary princes not only deserted the Imperial standard on that critical occasion, but superadded the crimes of revolt and usurpation. They established petty principalities; and, like the Captains of Alexander, governed by cruelty the dominions which they had acquired by treason. Such was the origin of those traitors, who are at present dignified by the appellation of Princes of India.

The character of Nizam-ul-muluc, who betrayed his master, has been the theme of universal execration; and the remnant of perfidious Nabobs, many of whom suffered from the chaos of destruction

tion which their treasons brought on the Empire, merit no better reputation.

When we hear or read poetical orations on the delinquencies of India, we ought never to forget, that the greatest delinquents are the native princes. The simplicity and innocence of the inhabitants of Indostan have been a frequent theme of declamation, but, like other topics of a similar nature, have no foundation in truth. " In cunning, treachery, and perfidy," said Mr. Dundas, after his enquiries into the affairs of the East, " no European is a match for an Indian. In oppression and cruelty the same character is predominant. The feelings of Britain have not yet forgot the shocking cruelties practised in the black hole at Calcutta, when hundreds of our countrymen perished in the most excruciating agonies, by hunger, thirst, and suffocation—because the slumbers of the Nabob were not to be disturbed! The fate of General Matthews, and his officers, at Syringpatnam, is fresh in the memory of of England. The inhuman tortures which they suffered in prison; the horrid deaths to which they were condemned; and the atrocious cruelties committed on their dead bodies, are scenes that would make an Inquisitor tremble; and over them I shall draw a veil, for the sake of human nature. When acting against persons of this character and description, wisdom as well as virtue will dictate the prevention of evil, rather than its remedy; and a temporary severity may be the most enlarged and liberal humanity.

3. In estimating the character, and pronouncing concerning the conduct of a Governor of Indostan, we are to consider the sovereign power, whose minister he is, and whose person he represents. A company of merchants, possessing extensive dominions, and at the head of a great empire on the opposite extremity of the globe, opens a new scene in human affairs. No laws nor precedents apply to a situation which is without a parallel in the history of past

past ages. We are not to expect, that the maxims of commercial policy will be the most liberal and enlarged; nor that the spirit of mercantile sovereignty will be the most heroic and generous. The government of provinces, situated at such an immense distance, must always be unfavourable to the subject, as the object of the legislators must necessarily be to monopolize the produce of the country, and convert the labours of the people to their own emolument and advantage. Such it would be in a single monarch or an aristrocracy, much more in a mercantile republic. Acting in the double capacity of sovereigns and merchants, the character of the latter will ever predominate over that of the former. Mercantile habits and associations draw them, in a natural and insensible manner, to grasp the present at the expence of the future, and to prefer the transient profits of the monopolist, to the permanent revenue of the prince. Considered as sovereigns, the interest of the India Company coincides with that of the provinces

vinces which they govern; confidered as merchants, it is frequently oppofite, as prefent gain is preferred to future advantage.

Treating on thefe fubjects, the moft ingenious and profound philofopher of the prefent age, whofe luminous intellect is only excelled by the perfect probity of his heart, thus expreffes his fentiments*:

" I mean not, by what I have faid, to throw any odious imputation upon the general character of the fervants of the Eaft-India-Company, and much lefs upon that of any particular perfons. It is the fyftem of government, the fituation in which they are placed, that I mean to cenfure; not the character of thofe who have acted in it: they acted as their fituation naturally directed; and they *who have clamoured the loudeft againft them*, would, probably, *not have acted better themfelves.* In war and negociation, the councils of Bengal, Madras, and Calcutta, have, upon

* Dr. Smith's Treatife on the Wealth of Nations, vol. ii. p. 484.

several occasions, conducted themselves with a resolution and decisive mind, which would have done honour to the Senate of Rome in the best days of that Republic. The members of those councils, however, had been bred to professions very different from war and politics; but their situation alone, without education, experience, or even example, seems to have formed in them all at once the great qualities which it required, and to have inspired them both with abilities and virtues, which they themselves could not well know they possessed. If, upon some occasions, it has animated them to actions of magnanimity which could not have been well expected from them, we should not wonder that upon others it has prompted them to exploits of somewhat a different nature."

Mr. Burke, in his speech on Mr. Fox's India bill, expresses his sentiments still more strongly: " *All the mischiefs in the East,*" says he, " *originated with the Company,* which is so constituted as not to admit the Governor General to be an *upright man.*

There is nothing worfe in the boys we fend to India, than in the boys whom we are whipping at fchool, or that we fee trailing a pike, or bending over a defk at home." Although this fentiment is expreffed with that rhetorical exaggeration which diftinguifhes Mr. Burke, even among modern orators; it conveys this important truth, that effential defects are connected with the nature of our Indian government, and that if any mal-adminiftration takes place, it is to be charged to the Company at home, not to their Reprefentative abroad.

If the fituation of a reprefentative of the India Company, in their foreign dominions, be at all times attended with difficulties almoft infurmountable, thefe verged on impoffibility during the adminiftration of Mr. Haftings. When the royal revenues of Bengal came into the poffeffion of the Company, a romantic expectation arofe of inexhauftible treafure from thefe new acquired fources of wealth. Intoxicated with fuch golden dreams, the minifters and the Company were alike folicitous

citous to obtain large annual remittances from thefe new-opened veins of opulence in India. In the fecond year after the acquifition of the Duanee, the Englifh government induced the Company to engage for the annual payment of 400,000 l. as a divifion to the public of the fuperfluous opulence of Bengal. This inconfiderate and inordinate avarice of the public, was the origin of all the evils which followed.

It is not, however, now a matter of aftonifhment to any reflecting mind, that the Court of Directors fhould have been fo deceived. Lord Clive, in the year 1765, ftated the importance of his new acquifitions infinitely too high. An empire was at his command. The unfortunate Shaw Allum, the defcendant of Tamerlane, depended upon the reprefentative of a Company of Britifh Merchants for his daily bread. Sujah Dowlah, Nabob of Oude, and Vizier of the empire of Indoftan, was compelled to throw himfelf upon the mercy of thofe whom he could no longer oppofe in the field. His Lordfhip dictated the terms of peace to both, and they were eagerly and gratefully accepted. To the Mogul he gave the provinces of Corah, Currah, and Allahabad, as a royal demefne for the fupport of his dignity; to which he added twenty-fix lacks of rupees from the revenues of Bengal. In return the Mogul gave to the Company, what the Company was then in poffeffion of; a kingdom they had conquered. To Sujah Dowlah Lord Clive reftored all his dominions, of which Benares was a part. To the Nabob of Bengal he gave an annual penfion of five hundred and fifty thoufand pounds; and after thefe deductions, the Company poffeffed the revenues and the adminiftration of Bengal. His Lordfhip took no merit for thefe acquifitions; but he reprefented their importance to the Company in terms too flattering. The amount of the revenues of Bengal, Bahar, and Oriffa, was magnified much beyond their actual produce; the expenditure was as much below the ftandard at which it ought to have been ftated. " I fhall," fays his Lordfhip, " after paying the ftipend to the

the Mogul and the Nabob, have sufficient to answer all your expences in Bengal, civil and military; to furnish Madras, Bombay, and China, with supplies of specie; to remit home large annual investments; nor will I draw upon your treasury in England for a shilling." With such a representation before them, was it extraordinary that Ministers, Proprietors, and Directors grew mad? Flattering as this picture was, some men in England became still more sanguine than Lord Clive. Mr. Holwell, I believe, stated the revenues of Bengal at nearly 10,000,000l. sterling.

In a few years the bubble burst; and when Mr. Hastings was appointed Governor of Bengal, in April 1772, he found that the investments of the two preceding years had been provided by drawing bills upon the Court of Directors for 1,200,000l. and by contracting a bonded debt to a greater amount in Bengal: and now a new delusion prevailed; it was confidently said, that the Company were defrauded of their revenues by the intrigues of Mahomed

homed Reza Cawn, and the Zemindars of Bengal. Mr. Haſtings' firſt inſtructions were, to deprive the former of all truſt, to ſeize his perſon, and to let the lands in farm. The reſult of an accurate and impartial examination into the conduct of Mahomed Reza Cawn, was his full and honourable acquittal; and as to the revenues, it was found that, after aboliſhing ſome very odious and oppreſſive taxes, no increaſe of revenue could be procured from Bengal. From what ſources then was relief to come? From none but thoſe which Mr. Haſtings created. He broke no treaty; he waged no wanton wars. After regulating the Government of Bengal with the ſtricteſt œconomy, he determined to improve our alliance with Sujah Dowlah; he withheld the annual ſtipend from the Mogul, becauſe that unhappy prince had deſerted our intereſts, and relinquiſhed our protection; he reſumed the government of thoſe provinces which the Mogul, on deſerting, had ceded to the Marhattas; he aſſiſted Sujah Dowlah in a war occaſioned by a groſs breach of a public treaty; we mean

mean the Rohilla war. By thefe acts he procured about two millions fterling for the Company in two years. And on the 18th of October, 1774, Mr. Haftings's adminiftration ended. For the two following years he was conftantly in a minority. The firft political act of the majority, Meffrs. Clavering, Monfon, and Francis, was one of the moft flagrant breaches of public faith ever known in any country; yet Mr. Burke has paffed it filently over, and it received the warmeft approbation of the King's Minifters and the Court of Directors. Far be it from me to throw a reflection upon the memory of thofe who are now no more; but in fpeaking of Mr. Haftings, can we forget that he ftrongly protefted againft the *only* breach of faith which was committed by the Government of Bengal during his adminiftration? What was the conduct of the Court of Directors, and what were their fentiments on this extraordinary occafion? "We think," fay they, in a letter dated in December 1775, " with our Governor General, that the treaty of alliance between us and the Nabob

bob Sujah Dowlah, did not expire at his death." But in a subsequent letter they add, " we rejoice that such important advantages have been obtained for the Company from his succeſsor; and we thank the majority for their attention to our intereſts." Theſe letters had the ſanction of the Treaſury while Lord North was the Miniſter.

Let me now turn the attention of my readers to the weſt of India, in order to ſee how far Mr. Haſtings is reſponſible for breach of faith in his tranſactions with the Marattas. It had long been a favourite idea with the moſt reſpectable men in the Direction, that a revenue ought to be procured in the neighbourhood of Bombay, ſufficient to meet the expences of that Government; upon this principle orders were iſſued to the Governor and Council of Bombay in 1768, to procure, if poſſible, the iſland of Salſette from the Marattas, but to do it rather by purchaſe than war. —" Get money, my ſon," ſaid the old man, " honeſtly if you can; but get money."

—So

—So said the Court of Directors. In the month of January 1775, the Bombay Government did take Salsette, under a pretence that the Portugueze meditated an attack upon that island. In March 1775, the same Government did precisely what Mr. Pitt and the King of Prussia are at this moment doing with so much eclat in Holland. They sided with Ragonaut Row, formerly the Peshwa of the Maratta state, against the Minister who had expelled him. A fairer opportunity never was offered for carrying every point which the Directors wanted; and it was justifiable by the practice of all states. The superior Council of Bengal, however, were unanimous in disapproving the conduct of the gentlemen of Bombay; Mr. Hastings condemned it as unauthorised and impolitic, tending to consequences which no man could foresee; but the deed being done, he advised that the future conduct of the Government of Bengal should be determined by circumstances, and that the orders to Bombay should be in some measure discretional.

Not so the majority, Messrs. Clavering, Monson, and Francis; they proclaimed aloud to all India, that the Bombay Government had acted wrong; and they sent an ambassador to Poona to declare as much to them, and to conclude a peace. The ambassador, Colonel Upton, said, on his arrival, that the English might command a peace, all the independent Chiefs of the Maratta state waiting to see the part which they should act. A peace was made and signed the first of April 1776; and for nineteen months the Supreme Council vainly endeavoured to enforce the execution of the articles. In fact, not one of them was executed; and the Maratta Ministers, foreseeing that a war must ensue, applied for assistance to France, which was solemnly promised them.

The Directors, in concert with the King's Ministers, expressed the highest satisfaction at the capture of Salsette; and were as much pleased to find the cause of Ragonaut Row so warmly espoused; but in proportion

tion as they looked forward with hope to their favourite object, were they disappointed when they heard of the interference of the Bengal Government, and the peace of Poorunder. They lamented that the interests of the Company had been sacrificed by that peace; and they authorised a renewal of the engagements with Ragonaut Row, if any article of the late treaty should remain unfulfilled. Every subsequent measure taken by Mr. Hastings in the Maratta war, was approved by the Directors: both knew the designs of the French upon India; and both knew that it was absolutely necessary for us to resist so dangerous an alliance. Every step that human wisdom or foresight could suggest, was taken to prevent the war in the Carnatic. When it broke out with such alarming appearances, the superior genius of Mr. Hastings alone stemmed the torrent of our ill success, and dissolved that confederacy which had been professedly formed for our destruction.

In stating the conduct of the Court of Directors, I mean not to condemn any part
of

of it. The whole was strictly consonant to the practice of all states in all ages; and in truth, they acted in concurrence with, and under the controul of the King's Ministers throughout all the late war. If the engagements with Ragonaut Row are condemned, upon what principle shall the support of the Stadtholder be justified? Tell not me, said Mr. Fox, speaking like a man, of the constitution of Holland; I stop not to enquire about it. Two parties contend for the power of government; France supports the one, and it is our interest to protect the other.

In the war which Great Britain madly waged with France in 1756 in defence of America when on the eve of rebellion, it will ever be a doubtful point which party was the aggressor. It was carried on with circumstances of cruelty far exceeding any thing we read of in India. Both parties employed the savages of America. Was there ever so inhuman, I had almost said so diabolical an act as the removal of the peaceful,

peaceful, unoffending French neutrals from Acadia, at the commencement of that war? Both were juftified on the plea of neceffity. Did not France exclaim againft us in every court of Europe, for feizing her fhips in time of profound peace? yet the meafure was a laudable one. In vain, however, do I fearch through the hiftory of the Britifh tranfactions in India for acts of this complexion.

4. In forming our opinion concerning the wifdom or impropriety, the equity or injuftice, of any government or adminiftration, we ought to attend to the eftablifhed maxims of authority confirmed by former precedents. Suppofing, for a moment, that the accufations brought againft Mr. Haftings are as agreeable to truth as they are founded on mifreprefentation, they amount to no more than this, that he fometimes exercifed the power committed to him, more agreeably to Afiatic than European ideas, but exercifed it for the moft

most salutary purposes, to preserve the dominions committed to his charge. Instructions from the Court of Directors, and orders from the House of Commons, may have been sent to India, and neglected or disobeyed from the same beneficent maxims by which they were dictated. Unless the House of Commons arrogate OMNISCIENCE as well as OMNIPOTENCE, it ought not to prescribe the tenor of transactions in an unknown country, where decisions must be formed on the pressure of the occasion; nor attempt to regulate the events of a contingent futurity. In such situations, according to the maxim of Eastern wisdom, " A man's own mind will tell him more than seven sages that sit on a high tower." Ever since the British standard has been erected in Indostan, the genius of our administration, conformable to the governments of the country, has been imperious and austere, rather than smiling and serene.

Our

Our possessions in Asia were gained by the sword, and, if they are to be retained, must in all future ages be held by the sword.

In the administration of Mr. Hastings, there is no act imputed to him that is not authorised by former examples and established precedents. How is the government of any country to be known and ascertained, but by ancient forms and immemorial practice? All laws, in their commencement, were merely consuetudinary, and founded on that experience which is dictated by the common sense of mankind. Every code of legislation, in every corner of the world, is established on previous usages and hereditary habits. There is not a single or solitary fact in the government of Mr. Hastings, that has not a sanction or example in the administration of Lord Clive.

It is on this principle that the Royal family of Stuart have been fully vindicated by by the retrospect of history, and justified to the conscience of mankind. They only attempted to retain and transmit undiminished and unimpaired, the powers and prerogatives which had been hereditary in the house of Tudor. The state of the kingdom, the situation and the sentiments of the people, had changed; but every principle which has hitherto actuated the masters of mankind, gives its sanction to the maxims which they pursued, to maintain the dignity, and support the privileges, which descended to them from their predecessors. The success of the grand rebellion served only to render the crimes of the conspirators more flagrant; the trial, sentence, and condemnation of Charles the First has left an indelible and eternal disgrace on the character of Britain. Is one century to renew the follies, and repeat the barbarities of another? While we blush for the misconduct, and tremble at the crimes of our fathers, shall we bequeath the same infamous legacy to future generations?

There

There is a principle of improvement and melioration in every conftitution or government; the obfervation and experience of former times enlighten and correct the following; and the voice of time gradually teaches more perfect leffons of wifdom. But legiflation has no retrofpect; new regulations extend only to the future, and turn no reverted afpect on the paft. If an attempt is made to introduce the Englifh conftitution among the Gentoos (an attempt as impoffible as it would be pernicious), thofe are exempted from its jurifdiction who acted under a different government, and from other maxims of policy. If a new SUN is to rife in the WEST, and fend its propitious ray to India, let not its dazzling fplendours confume the heads of thofe who acted in the fhade of former obfcurity.

5. Rewards and punifhments are the great engines of government, and the wife and proper adminiftration of them forms

the chief distinction between a good and a bad minister. There are particular occasions, when, from the manners of the times, remuneration of public merit, and retribution for national offences, become essentially necessary. At the commencement of a former war with France, when no zeal appeared among our commanders and officers in the service of their country, the punishment of Admiral Byng operated on the army and the navy like an electrical shock, brought all the valour of the kingdom into exertion, and led on to victory and conquest.

After a war so disastrous and disgraceful as the last, justice, as well as policy, might demand a victim to be sacrificed to the public resentment. If the Generals who accepted of their commission with an intention to betray their country, who fought the battles of America instead of the parent state, and delivered up armies into the hands of the enemy, had been impeached for having dismem-

dismembered the British dominions, and lost thirteen provinces to this empire, the feelings and reflections of the nation would perhaps have gone along with the measure. But to have harassed with persecutions and impeachments Admiral Rodney, and the Governor of Bengal, without whose splendid and meritorious exertions Britain would have read the last brilliant page of her history, and sunk into her primitive insignificance in the map of the world, is an insult to the common sense and spirit of the nation, and establishes a precedent that, in future times, must check the ardour and infrigidate the exertions of the executive branch of government: for it must occur to every person who is acquainted with political affairs, that if to all the *metaphysical* misdemeanors which have been imputed to Mr. Hastings, he had added one *real crime*, had thrown his weight into the scale of opposition, and violated the principles of duty and allegiance which he has ever maintained to his sovereign, the same broad shield

shield of patriotism which protected the American delinquents, would have covered the Governor of India from every hostile attack; his impeachment would have been as much unknown as that of Lord North; and his name and character transmitted without a stain to the most distant posterity. Has attachment to principle, has loyalty to the sovereign, become such a crime, as to cancel the merit and obliterate the services of thirty years? Is there no medium between forming a monstrous and immoral coalition, and becoming the subject of impeachment?

If success, in any degree, attends the designs of the accusers of Mr. Hastings, the voice of Britain henceforth to her sons is, " Go and serve your country, but if you transgress the line of official orders, though compelled by necessity, you do so at the risque of your fortune, your honour, and your life; if you act with *proper prudence* against the interests of the empire, and bring

bring calamity and disgrace upon your country, you have only to court opposition, and coalesce with your enemies, and you will find a party zealous and devoted to support you; you may obtain a vote of thanks from the House of Commons for your *services*, and you may *read your history in the eyes of the mob* by the light of bonfires and illuminations. But if, after exerting all your efforts in the cause of your country, you return covered with laurels, and crowned with success; if you preserve a loyal attachment to your sovereign, you may expect the thunders of parliamentary vengeance; you will certainly be impeached, and probably be undone."

No government can exist on such maxims of policy. An administration so unprincipled and improvident as to make it an object to reward its enemies and punish its friends, contains within itself the principles of destruction. Such a mass of incoherent and discordant materials must soon be dissolved.

6. The

6. The principles from which men act in public life, stamp merit or demerit on their actions. If we can trace their conduct to disappointed ambition, personal resentment, or envy of superior worth, no pretensions to philanthropy or patriotism will vindicate their character in the view of an impartial public. The first great man whose impeachment is recorded in history was Miltiades, who had refused the sovereignty of Chersonesus, in order to establish the liberty of his country; and who, by gaining the victory of Marathon, gave an elevation to the character of the Athenians, which in every subsequent age rendered them superior to the Persians. The glory which he had acquired, in diminishing the consequence, excited the envy, of the Alemeonidæ; the security of the commonwealth, procured by his extraordinary abilities, rendered those abilities less necessary; and his accidental failure at Paros afforded means of accomplishing his ruin with a fickle multitude possessed of absolute authority. The Chief of the opposite faction

faction conducted a capital accusation against him; he was condemned in a fine of fifty talents, which he was unable to pay; and languished out the remains of a glorious life in the confinement and ignominy of a prison.

Among the conspirators against Cæsar, there was a single Brutus, who loved his country; but a multitude of personal foes, who sought only to gratify their private resentment by the assassination of the Dictator. The *honourable men*, who first conspired against the Governor of India, have happily furnished a key to their own character. Disappointed of empire in the East, by the failure of Mr. Fox's celebrated bill, they meditated revenge; and as their ambitious projects had been strongly resisted by the East India Company, they fixed upon their favourite servant, whom they had formerly accused, as an object of persecution and impeachment. Will it add to the credit of any faction, that they have forfeited the approbation and the confidence of their country? Will it serve as a recommendation to any cause, that the arch-accuser of Mr. Hastings was the apologist of Powel and Bembridge? Or will it add to the credibility of his present charges, that, after having accused Lord North of crimes that could *only be expiated on the public scaffold*, and drawn up articles of impeachment against him, he now employs that very hand to crown him with laurels, which was formerly armed for his destruction? Does the addition of the name of a celebrated General to the Committee of impeachment, reflect any lustre on their cause? A general who, in June 1777, according to his own statement, " gave a war-feast to the Indians, according to their own custom;" that is, authorised their horrid ceremony of drinking human blood out of the skulls of their enemies; who gave them his sanction to mangle the bodies of the slain, and take the scalps of the dead; who, in a proclamation written by himself, talks of "*giving a stretch to the Indian forces, of executing the vengeance of the state, of the messengers*

messengers of wrath, of devastation, famine, and every concomitant horror;" and who, after this pompous *prologue* of tragic ferocity, known only to the most savage of the American tribes, signed the fatal and ignominious convention at Saratoga, which drew France and Spain to the assistance of America, and deprived us of one half of our empire. The *youthful virtue* of Mr. Anstruther will not soon be forgotten; who, after having declared in a full Court of Proprietors, " That Mr. Hastings possessed two of the most essential requisites of a Governor, undoubted ability and undoubted integrity; and that he had made exertions during the war which exceeded belief," in a few years afterwards became a member and a manager of the committee of impeachment, and took as zealous and active a part against Mr. Hastings, as he had formerly done in his favour. The inconsistent and contradictory character of Mr. Francis is hardly an object of criticism. The personal enemy of Mr. Hastings ought to have been silent in a cause that was submitted

submitted to the decision of justice, not the dictates of animosity; nor ought he to have added to the reproach and ridicule he has already incurred from the world, by constantly attending the meetings of the Secret Committee, from which he was excluded by the House of Commons.

The *motives* from which this impeachment originated are farther illustrated by the manner in which it has been carried into execution. As it began, so it has been conducted, with that violent animosity and vindictive spirit, which seeks to blast the character of an individual; not by that cool sense of justice and equity which is solicitous only to vindicate the honour of the nation. Instead of fair and candid reasoning, his accusers have had recourse to satire, ridicule, and buffoonery; and have loaded with invectives and reproaches, unworthy at all times to be heard in the British Senate, and fit only to be applied to the most atrocious criminal after conviction, a personage pronounced innocent by the law till

till he is found guilty, and placed in a situation, which, from its eminence alone, entitled him to respect and veneration. This is a language which truth disclaims; these are weapons which virtue disowns. There is a difference between the stroke of justice and the stab of an assassin.

The office of calm deliberate justice is to redress grievances, as well as to punish offences. It has been affirmed, that the natives of India have been deeply injured; but has any motion been made to make them compensation for the injuries they have sustained? Have the accusers of Mr. Hastings ever proposed to bring back the Rohillas to the country from which they were expelled? to restore Cheit Sing to the Zemindary of Benares? or to return to the Nabob of Oude the present which the Governor of Bengal received from him for the benefit of the Company? Till such measures are adopted, and in the train of negociation, the world has every reason to conclude, that the impeachment of Mr. Hastings

Hastings is carried on from motives of personal animosity, not from regard to public justice.

In turning my attention to the other side of the House of Commons, I shall only state a few facts. In 1785, Mr. Dundas expressed his astonishment at the manner by which Mr. Hastings discovered or created resources during the war; "but by these means," says he, "he has saved India. I approved of his receiving the thanks of the Directors; and had I been a Director, I would have joined most heartily in that vote." The same Mr. Dundas, in 1786, gave his vote to impeach Mr. Hastings for the identical conduct on which he had formerly pronounced a panegyric.

Mr. George Hardinge expressed his opinion of Mr. Hastings at the bar of the House of Lords in the most animated and glowing terms. "Long the servant of the Company, Mr. Hastings has lived but for them, and for the Public united with them. What

What is the *real* character of this wonderful man? He is the Chatham of the East; an equal spirit of enterprize, the same resource, commanding genius, enlarged conceptions, and purity of character, will make both of them the idols of posterity, when *their little adversaries will be too obscure* for infamy to record them." If these gentlemen have since taken a different tone, it is not from any new discoveries that have been made; the reports of the Select Committee were published at the period when those Members of Parliament defended the cause of Mr. Hastings; and if since that time they have received a new light, it must have come through some medium unknown to the public.

The conduct of the Minister on this occasion, has been covered with a cloud, which no ray of reasoning can disperse, and involved in a labyrinth which no thread of argument can unwind. In the first, and in appearance the heaviest, charge brought against Mr. Hastings, he acquitted him by his vote. In the celebrated debate concerning

cerning the transactions at Benares, he described Mr. Hastings as one of the first men this country has produced; vindicated him in every step of his conduct towards Cheit Sing, whose obstinacy he criminated in the strongest terms; and at the same time found him liable to impeachment for an error in judgment, in which his greatest enemies discerned no trace of blame. In the question concerning the Begums, he advanced the gross and monstrous position, that rebels ought to be tried by law, and denied the existence of the state-necessity, which had been proved by Major Scott, from the evidence of authentic records. In the other debates, he alternately mixed the highest panegyric with the most poignant severities. At one time he extolled Mr. Hastings, as having preserved an empire to Great Britain, and saved a nation from perishing by famine. At another time, he poured forth the pathos of apparent compassion over the misfortunes of a man who had incurred the censure of the House of Commons. The reprimand

reprimand which he gave to Lord Hood, for expressing the manly sentiments of a gallant officer; his vindication of the low and indecent ribaldry employed by some of the enemies of Mr. Hastings, certainly excited no small degree of astonishment, both within the House, and amongst the Public. On these facts I shall make no commentary, but leave the reader to his own reflections.

Whatever conjectures may be formed in consequence of the warm panegyrics, and the harsh censures which the same men have, at different periods, heaped upon Mr. Hastings; whether the one or the other, or both, are to be attributed to private interest, to caprice, to disappointed ambition, or to momentary passion; whether men who have been deprived of comfortable sinecures, in which they thought themselves secure for life, attribute their misfortunes to the late Governor General of Bengal, and are actuated by private revenge; whether, as Mr. Sheridan once said, certain men feel a pleasure in humbling the man by whose
assistance

assistance (if Opposition is to be believed) they defeated a very powerful party; whether those who have carried the impeachment to the Lords were actuated by any of these motives, it is now of no moment to enquire. Every friend of Mr. Hastings and of humanity, will rejoice that his cause is carried before a tribunal competent to his acquittal, or his condemnation; and the nation will look with confidence on the deliberative wisdom, and impartial justice, which will dictate the decision of the most august tribunal upon earth.

FINIS.

The following BOOKS *are just published by* JOHN STOCKDALE, Piccadilly, *and* JOHN MURRAY, Fleet-street.

1. A Dissertation on the Governments, Manners, and Spirit of Asia. By the Rev. Mr. Logan. Price 1s. 6d.

2. Essays

2. Essays on Hunting: containing a Philosophical Enquiry into the Nature and Properties of the Scent; and Observations on the different Kinds of Hounds, with the Manner of training them. Also, Directions for the Choice of a Hunter; the Qualifications requisite for a Huntsman; and other General Rules to be observed in every Contingency incident to the Chace. With an Introduction, describing the Method of Hare Hunting, practised by the Greeks. A new Edition: With a Supplement, containing an Account of the Vizier's Manner of Hunting in the Mogul Empire. By William Blane, Esq. In one Volume 8vo. Price 4s. in Boards.

3. Articles exhibited by the Knights, Citizens, and Burgesses in Parliament assembled, in the Name of themselves and of all the Commons of Great-Britain, against WARREN HASTINGS, Esq. late Governor General of Bengal, in maintenance of their Impeachment against him for High Crimes and Misdemeanors, (WITH THE AMENDMENTS.) Price 2s. 6d.

4. The Answer of Warren Hastings, Esq. to the Articles exhibited by the Knights, Citizens, and Burgesses in Parliament assembled, in the name of themselves, and of all the Commons of Great-Britain, in maintenance of their Impeachment against him for High Crimes and Misdemeanors, supposed to have been by him committed. Delivered at the Bar of the House of Peers, on Wednesday, November 28, 1787. In one Volume 8vo. Price only 4s. in Boards.

5. Articles of Charge of High Crimes and Misdemeanors against Warren Hastings, Esq. presented to the House of Commons by the Right Hon. Edmund Burke. In one large Volume 8vo. Price 7s. in Boards.

6. The Defence of Warren Hastings, Esq. (late Governor General of Bengal,) at the Bar of the House of Commons, upon the Matter of the several Charges

of High Crimes and Misdemeanors, presented against him in the Year 1786. In one Volume 8vo. Price 5s. in Boards.

7. Minutes of the Evidence taken before a Committee of the House of Commons, being a Committee of the Whole House, appointed to consider of the several Articles of Charge of High Crimes and Misdemeanors presented to the House against Warren Hastings, Esq. late Governor General of Bengal: Containing the Examinations of Sir Robert Barker, Bart. Colonel Champion; Major Marsack; Captain Leonard Jacques; Major Balfour; Major Gardener; Major Gilpin; Nathaniel Middleton, Esq. Captain Williams; Sir Elijah Impey; Captain Thomas Mercer; William Young, Esq. Mr. Isaac Baugh; William Harwood, Esq. Ewan Law, Esq. Alexander Higginson, Esq. Peter Moore, Esq. William Markham, Esq. David Anderson, Esq. Mr. William Wright. In one large Volume 8vo. Price 7s. 6d. in Boards.

8. A Narrative of the Insurrection which happened in the Zemeedary of Benares, in the Month of August 1781, and of the Transactions in that District; with an Appendix of authentic Papers and Affidavits. By Warren Hastings, Esq.

9. The Present State of the East-Indies, by Warren Hastings, Esq. late Governor General of Bengal; with Notes by the Editor. Price only 2s.

10. Articles of Charge of High Crimes and Misdemeanors, against Sir Elijah Impey, Knt. late Chief Justice of the Supreme Court of Judicature at Fort William, in Bengal, presented to the House of Commons, upon the 12th Day of December, 1787, by Sir Gilbert Elliot, Bart. Price 2s. 6d.

11. Minutes of Warren Hastings and Philip Francis, Esquires, relative to their personal Quarrel. Price 1s. 6d.

12. Mr.

12. Mr. Sheridan's Speech on the Charges brought against Mr. Haſtings. Price 3s.

13. The Debate on the Rohilla War, in the Houſe of Commons, the 1ſt and 2d of June 1786, Price 1s. 6d.

14. The Debate on the Charge relative to Mr. Haſtings's Conduct to Cheyt Sing, at Benares, in the Houſe of Commons, on the 13th of June, 1786. Price 1s.

15. The Debate in the Houſe of Commons, June 25th, 1786, on the Eaſt-India Relief Bill, in which is included the Hiſtory of the Diamond delivered to Lord Sydney by Major John Scott. Price 1s.

16. The Bengal Calendar, for the Year 1788: Including a Liſt of the Honourable and United Eaſt-India Company's Civil and Military Servants on the Bengal Eſtabliſhment, &c. Including alſo thoſe at Madras, Bombay, Fort Marlborough, China, and St. Helena. A new Edition. Corrected at the Eaſt-India Houſe. Price 1s. 6d. ſewed in Marble Paper.

17. The London Calendar, or Court and City Regiſter for England, Scotland, Ireland, and America, for the Year 1788, including a complete and correct Liſt of the preſent Parliament, &c. &c. &c. more extenſive and uſeful than in any other Book of the Kind yet publiſhed. Carefully corrected at the reſpective Offices. Printed on a large Paper. Price only 1s. 6d. ſewed, or 2s. bound.

⁎ The above Calendar may be had complete with the New Heraldry in Miniature, containing the Arms of the Peers and Baronets: Almanack, Companion, and Bengal Calendar, bound together. Price 8s.

N. B. Be careful to aſk for the London Calendar.

18. Field-

18. Fielding's New Peerage of England, Scotland, and Ireland, for 1788; containing the Origin and Progress of Honours, Manner of creating Peers, Order of Knighthood, Introduction to Heraldry, with an Heraldic Dictionary, and a complete Extinct Peerage. In a neat Pocket Volume. Price only 6s. in Boards, or 7s. 6d. Calf gilt.

⁎ The above New Edition of the Peerage is corrected to the present Time, and contains of Copper-plate and Letter-press 400 Pages, which is nearly double the Quantity of the last Edition, though the Price is not advanced to the Public.

19. New Heraldry in Miniature: Containing all the Arms, Crests, Supporters, and Mottos, of the Peers, Peeresses, and Bishops, of England, Scotland, and Ireland, with the Baronets of Great-Britain; and the Insignia of the different Orders of Knighthood in the Three Kingdoms: also an Introduction to the Science of Heraldry, a Dictionary of Heraldic Terms, as well as an Index to all the Peers, &c. with the Translation of their Mottos: Likewise a List of Titles conferred by his present Majesty, and those extinct since his Accession to the Throne. Containing upwards of 1000 Arms of the Peers and Baronets, and Rules of Precedency amongst Men and Women. Price only 2s. 6d. sewed in Marble Paper.

20. Remarks upon Colonel Fullarton's View of the English Interests in India. Dedicated to the Officers in the Service of the East-India Company in Bengal. By an Officer, late in the Company's Service in Bengal. Price 1s. 6d.

The Debates of the Last Session of the late Parliament, in Six Volumes, 8vo. Price 1l. 11s. 6d. half bound and lettered.

⁎ The above Six Volumes contain Mr. Pitt's and Mr. Fox's East-India Bills, and all the Debates on that Subject.

12. Also

21. Also the Debates for 1784, First Session of the present Parliament (being the 16th,) in Three large Volumes, 8vo. Price 1l. 1s. half bound and lettered.

22. Ditto 1785, Second Session, in Three Volumes, 8vo. Price 1l. 1s. half bound and lettered.

23. Debates in Parliament in 1786, Third Session, in Three Volumes, 8vo. Price 1l. 1s. half bound and lettered.

24. Ditto 1787, Fourth Session, in Three Volumes, 8vo. Price 1l. 1s. half bound and lettered.

⁎ The above Debates contain a very full Account of the Proceedings respecting Mr. Hastings, and the East-India Affairs.

25. The Tribunal, addressed to the Peers of Great-Britain about to sit in Judgment on Warren Hastings, Price 2s. 6d.

www.ingramcontent.com/pod-product-compliance
Lightning Source LLC
Chambersburg PA
CBHW022146160426
43197CB00009B/1445